Original title:
The Budding Bard

Copyright © 2025 Creative Arts Management OÜ
All rights reserved.

Author: Henry Beaumont
ISBN HARDBACK: 978-1-80567-063-6
ISBN PAPERBACK: 978-1-80567-143-5

Buds Unfurled in Rhyme

In the garden of words, a seed took flight,
Puns and giggles danced in the light.
Roses think they're clever with their thorny pranks,
While daisies plot poetry in colorful ranks.

Jokes sprout from petals, who knew they'd sing?
Even weeds join the chorus, looking for bling.
Chasing after rhymes, oh what a sight,
Blooming mischief beneath the moonlight.

Awakening the Quill

A quill woke up, with ink in its veins,
Scribbling nonsense, driving the world insane.
It wrote of a goat who wore fancy shoes,
Dancing on rooftops, singing the blues.

Birds laughed at the lines, they flew overhead,
A cat was a poet, quite full of dread.
With every stroke, the world turned bright,
Comedy flourished in the comical night.

Whispers of New Verses

Whispers of laughter in the words yet penned,
Bouncing along till the very end.
A snail with a monocle, oh so refined,
Critiquing the frogs that are too well-defined.

Tickling the pages with a fluffy feather,
Each word that is written just gets even better.
So if you hear giggles while flipping a book,
It's the verses themselves that are off on the hook.

Ink Blossoms

Inkwells blossom with stories untold,
Where squirrels recite sonnets, daring and bold.
A chipmunk steps up, wearing a hat,
Declaring the season for rhyme, imagine that!

Petals scatter lines, so silly and spry,
As bees join in chorus with a buzzing sigh.
What's life without laughter, a dance in the sun?
These whimsical verses are all in good fun.

Seeds of Song

In a garden where giggles sprout,
Tiny seeds begin to shout.
With whispers of melody in the breeze,
They dance like ants, bursting to tease.

Wiggly worms join the fun parade,
With rhymes that make flowers feel swayed.
Each joke around, a petal will shake,
As taffy rolls in to join the lake.

Frogs croak lines, bubbling with glee,
While bees make a buzz — oh so free!
Sing to the clouds that are fluffy and white,
With laughter as bright as the stars at night.

The Voice of Young Roots

Down below where the giggles grow,
Roots are chatting, not moving slow.
With whispers heard through the soil's embrace,
They craft little verses, a funny place!

Grumpy stones with their serious face,
Try to join in, but just lose the race.
And mushrooms, round with caps so wide,
Snicker at roots who can't even glide.

Above, the flowers burst out in cheer,
As wild tunes tickle the world they steer.
With each little word, a chuckle arises,
Soon the sun joins in with its bright surprises.

Poetic Ripples in Bloom

A pond reflects a humorous scene,
With ducks in hats — quite the routine!
They quack out verses, what a delight,
While lilies gossip throughout the night.

The frogs leap high, trying to rhyme,
With splashy lines, they make up their chime.
Little fish giggle and wiggle in joy,
As the water plays tunes with a shiny toy.

Each ripple that dances starts a new tune,
Creating a melody beneath the moon.
In a world where laughter is always in bloom,
Nature spins yarns that erase all gloom.

The First Stanza

Once upon a time, in a land so silly,
A poet found joy in a dancing willy-nilly.
With a pen in hand and a grin on his face,
He wrote down his thoughts to quicken the pace.

Each word was a step, a wiggly prance,
As he jotted down notes in a summer dance.
With comic relief tucked in every line,
He crafted his stanzas, oh how they shine!

The trees leaned in, curious to hear,
As squirrels applauded, showering cheer.
For in every laugh, a lesson was spun,
The first stanza ended, but the fun's just begun!

Inked Horizons

A feathered pen danced in glee,
As I scribbled my joy, wild and free.
Lines twisted and leaped with delight,
Words became birds, taking flight.

My ink pot spilled like a puddle,
Oh, what chaos! A marvelous muddle.
They say clean up is a bore,
But I found poems hiding galore!

Each stanza dripped with giggles and grins,
Even the paper, where mischief begins.
I wore ink stains like badges of pride,
Writer's block laughed, but I just sighed.

With humor in mind, I crafted my tale,
Of wizards and pirates, in a daring scale.
The horizon gleamed with stories untold,
Inked secrets waiting to unfold.

Flourishing Stanzas

My rhymes pranced like frogs on a log,
Each word a giggle, or maybe a hog.
In a world bursting with color and cheer,
I penned my dreams, sipping on beer.

Lines sprouted legs, took off on a spree,
They waltzed on the page, dancing with glee.
One stanza tripped, and a poem fell down,
It got up with a laugh, wearing a crown.

The moon joined in with a cheeky grin,
Lighting the path where laughter begins.
Ink spilled from my heart, flowing like wine,
Each flourish a jest, a playful design.

I rolled on the floor, papers afloat,
Chasing my muse on a bright red boat.
The stanzas grew wings, oh what a sight!
With humor at helm, they soared into the night.

The First Taps of Inspiration

A tap on my shoulder, a nudge from fate,
Ideas tickled me, oh wasn't it great?
I blinked at the page, a comedy scene,
Where blankness just laughed, it knew what I mean.

With a plop and a pop, my thoughts came alive,
Like ants on a picnic, they thrashed and they thrived.
I juggled my quill, balancing words,
While giggling at sentences, flying like birds.

Then came a chorus, a tune I hum,
A symphony built on the sound of my bum!
I wrote of a frog who wished to be king,
Each sentence a ribbit, the joy it would bring.

Inspiration was ticklish, it made me chuckle,
As laughter exploded like warm, gooey muckle.
With rhythm and rhyme, I conquered the night,
Juggling lines, oh what a delight!

Emergence of Expression

Out of the shadows, my silliness crept,
With each quirky line, laughter adept.
Like a magician, I waved my pen bright,
Words popped from nowhere, what a funny sight!

I scrambled for verses, they scattered like spark,
Chasing the whimsy that ignited the dark.
In a theater of nonsense, my ideas took shape,
As clowns in the audience began to escape.

With characters slipping on banana peels,
Every line shimmered with laughter that heals.
A troupe of misfits danced on the stage,
In the spotlight of folly, they flew from the page.

Pen in my hand, I embraced the absurd,
Expressions of joy rushed forth, undeterred.
The ink flowed like laughter, filling the air,
In the emergence of fun, my heart laid bare.

Sprouts of Expression

A sprout of thought, it wriggles and shakes,
Words without rhyme? Oh, what a mistake!
They dance on the page, in quite the parade,
With giggles and wiggles, they're not even afraid.

Puns sprout like daisies, a garden of glee,
Tangled in laughter, come join the spree!
A joke here, a pun there, all in good cheer,
With every new line, we're ready, my dear!

Like mushrooms at night, ideas pop up,
Fill the pages with whimsy, let's fill up our cup!
Quirky and funny, our words take flight,
In this jolly jungle, we soar with delight!

So raise up a toast to our silly little scripts,
In the land of the laughing, we throw joyful quips!
With each silly stanza, our spirits will lift,
In the garden of giggles, we've found our great gift.

Harbingers of Hidden Stories

A whispering breeze tells tales yet untold,
Of frogs in tuxedos and pirates so bold!
In shadows and giggles, they frolic and play,
With punchlines galore, they brighten the day.

There's a cat on a kettle, cooking up dreams,
With muffins and magic, and sugary beams!
Join in the laughter, let spirits be bright,
As the stories uncover, in comedic delight.

Each word is a jester, each phrase is a clown,
With silly disguises, they twirl upside down!
Watch as they tumble and cheerfully caper,
In this realm of wonders, come grab your newspaper!

So gather around, for the tales that are spun,
From the quirk of the fables, we all have our fun!
With every new story, we share an embrace,
Like hiccups and chuckles, they fill up the space.

First Frost of Inspiration

A frosty morning, ideas sit tight,
With mittens of nonsense, they think of delight.
Fingers freezing, but laughter brings heat,
As wacky thoughts dance on the tips of our feet.

Snowflakes like punchlines, they tumble and fall,
Each landing a giggle, a whimsical call.
Our warm cups of joy overflow with good cheer,
As we pen all the frolics that tickle the ear.

We'll build a snowman from rather tall dreams,
With a carrot for a nose, or so it seems!
He tells us his secrets, all wrapped up in jest,
In the wintery dawn, we find we're all blessed.

So cherish the chill, and let laughter unfold,
With each frosty giggle, our stories grow bold!
Inspiration's first frost, like ice on our cheeks,
Brings whimsical wonders and humorous peaks.

A Symphony of New Beginnings

A tip-tap on the drums, a clap in the air,
With notes of absurdity, we dance without care.
The horns bellow loudly, a chorus of glee,
As we compose our laughter, let it flow free!

The string section twirls, a quirky ballet,
As cheeky characters join in the play.
With every crescendo, we giggle and sway,
In this lively orchestra, who needs to be gray?

A whimsical overture, a jolly refrain,
In this symphonic madness, we celebrate gain!
With flutes full of joy and clarinets bright,
Our laughter's the melody that fills up the night.

So let's raise our voices, let's sing with delight,
In this symphony silly, we shine like the light!
With rhythms of giggles, our spirits take wing,
In this joyous ensemble, let's dance and let sing!

Voices from the Garden

In the plot where shadows play,
Worms recite on a sunny day.
Carrots giggle, peas all cheer,
Sunflowers sway, the sky is clear.

Butterflies launch a grand ballet,
With ladybugs leading the fray.
Bees buzz jokes that fly and spin,
While seedlings chuckle, 'Let's begin!'

Rabbits debate the best green treat,
Hilarity grows with every beat.
A garden dance that won't grow old,
Where laughter blooms, and joy unfolds.

So grab your hat and join the fun,
In a garden where all is spun.
The flowers speak, their whims ablaze,
As nature hosts a merry craze.

Seedlings of Sentiment

Oh, dear seedlings with hearts so bright,
You whisper secrets in the night.
With every raindrop, tales begin,
Of love-struck roots and leaves in spin.

Petunias ponder who's the best,
While daisies play a game of jest.
Their giggles drift on soft, warm air,
As budding dreams are everywhere.

Buttercups blush at dawn's first glance,
Inviting bees to join the dance.
With rhymes that twirl beneath the sun,
Their leafy tales have just begun.

So tend your garden, watch it grow,
For every seed's got stories to show.
With laughter sprouting on every side,
In this patch of life, joy cannot hide.

Ink and Sap

In a ink-stained world where thoughts collide,
Trees whisper tales, branches open wide.
A squirrel named Quill pens a story grand,
While sap becomes the poet's band.

With tiny paws that write and scribble,
He captures dreams on paper, so dribble!
Bark-chewing ants lend a helping hand,
Creating verses, perfectly planned.

Underneath the canopy, words unfurl,
As wildflowers dance and twirl.
The ink of nature flows and drips,
While laughter echoes from playful quips.

So raise your pen, let thoughts take flight,
In the forest where humor feels just right.
With every drop of sap, a new reveal,
Creating art that all can feel.

The Poet's Awakening

When morning dew kisses sleepy buds,
A poet stirs from dreaming floods.
With butterflies whispering in his ear,
He crafts a sonnet, filled with cheer.

His rhymes dance like bees in the bloom,
While petals chuckle in vibrant room.
A frog croaks lines with endless glee,
Turning each lily into poetry.

With ink on fingers and a hat askew,
He scribbles humors in shades of blue.
Dandelions bow as he strums along,
Their seeds catch wind like a joyful song.

So celebrate this dawn, dear friend,
For laughter is the trend that won't end.
With each new verse, let joy take a stand,
And paint the world with a giggling hand.

Hopes Like Dandelions

In the breeze, dreams take flight,
Floating seeds, pure delight.
Chasing clouds, silly and fast,
Hoping one will bloom at last.

In the garden, weeds are grand,
Tickled by the sun's warm hand.
With a giggle, they spread wide,
Dandelions, our crazy pride.

Winds of change blow, spin around,
In this chaos, joy is found.
Sprouting laughter in every crack,
Wild and free, no looking back.

Tiny wishes whirl and dance,
Each one holds a quirky chance.
With a chuckle, we'll watch them rise,
Chasing dreams, beneath blue skies.

The Path of the Word Weaver

Stitching letters, with a grin,
Words like yarn, where to begin?
Knots of humor, tales that twirl,
Weaving stories, watch them whirl.

In a patchwork, giggles grow,
A tapestry of highs and lows.
Each rhyme a stitch, quite absurd,
Mirthful tracks where tales are heard.

With a needle made of dreams,
We craft life with silly schemes.
Puns and giggles, laughter's thread,
Creating joy with every spread.

As we wander, we'll not stray,
On this path, there's always play.
With each step, let humor lead,
In the garden of wordy seed.

Flourish and Flourish

Sprout a grin, let laughter grow,
With each giggle, joy will flow.
In this meadow, wild and bright,
Come dance with me till late at night.

From silly seeds, blossoms bloom,
Filling spaces, clearing gloom.
Frolic among the flowers' sway,
Chasing away the dull gray.

Petals bright, filled with cheer,
A riot of colors, loud and clear.
As we twirl and share a jest,
In this garden, we are blessed.

Every bloom, a joyful sound,
In this joke-filled patch, we're found.
So let's flourish, side by side,
In this world, let's take our ride.

Fledgling Revelations

Tiny thoughts begin to peek,
With a chuckle, dreams unique.
From the brink of silly lore,
We sprout ideas, wanting more.

Waddling like a duck on land,
Quirky plots, oh how they stand!
With each laugh, a secret spills,
In this wonder, joy fulfills.

Glimmers bright in playful minds,
With each ponder, humor binds.
Through the jest, the truth will show,
Fledgling thoughts, let giggles flow.

In the dance of whimsy's art,
Silly sparks ignite the heart.
Awake to laughter's sweet embrace,
In this world, we find our place.

Crafting the Unseen

In a world where puns take flight,
Words dance around, oh what a sight!
With giggles sprouting in the air,
I craft my verses, light as a chair.

Each syllable a playful tease,
A rhyme that hugs you like a sneeze.
I mix and match, all up in fun,
Underneath the quirky sun.

My quill is wild, my ink a prank,
On paper, chaos forms a plank.
With laughter weaving 'tween each line,
I sip my tea, and feel divine.

So here I stand, not one to fret,
My wordy antics, the best vignette.
With wit and whimsy, I'll evoke,
A giggle here, a chuckle stroke.

Lyrics Sprouting from the Soil

In gardens where the jokes do bloom,
Lyrics grow beneath the moon.
With roots of laughter, stems so bright,
Each line a flower, pure delight.

The daisies chuckle, roses blush,
While lilacs join in, oh what a rush!
I water puns with giggles sly,
Watch silly metaphors take to the sky.

Grab your shovel, let's dig deep,
In this soil, humor has no sleep.
We'll plant our thoughts with sprightly cheer,
And watch them grow, oh so near.

With playful rhymes, let's plant the fun,
A garden full of wordy run!
So come and join, don't plant alone,
In this lyrical patch, we've all grown.

The Songbirds' Narratives

In the trees where chatter sings,
Songbirds share their golden flings.
With every note and chirp they quirk,
They pen the tales of life's great perk.

One bird spoke of a shoe on a head,
While another recited lines from a bed.
With caws of laughter twirling 'round,
They spread their narratives profound.

With a rustle here, and a flap so grand,
These feathered bards have made their stand.
They'll tell your secrets, if they must,
With every tweet, a tale of trust.

So listen close to their quirky chats,
For wisdom lies in those feathery hats.
The songbirds' joy, a timeless tune,
Plays on repeat beneath the moon.

Revelations of the Greenheart

In forests lush, where giggles sprout,
The greenheart whispers, without a doubt.
With every leaf a tale it spins,
Of playful squirrels and cheeky wins.

Mossy floors hide secrets deep,
While mushrooms chuckle, half-asleep.
They dance around with roots entwined,
These ancient trees, so fun-designed.

With branches stretched, they share their breath,
Unveiling laughter, defying death.
In every shadow, a silly plot,
The greenheart's charm hits the spot.

So wander 'neath these leafy dreams,
Let the sunlight rush in, as it beams.
For here, amid the foliage bright,
Lies the revelation of pure delight.

New Growth, New Stories

A tiny sprout with dreams to share,
Wobbles on stage without a care.
It trips on roots, falls down with glee,
And shouts, "Look out! That's not just me!"

Leaves whisper secrets to the sun,
While earthworms giggle; oh, what fun!
If trees could laugh, they'd cheer it on,
But they just sway until it's gone.

The critters chuckle, and the buds bloom,
In this wild garden, there's always room.
For every tale that breaks the norm,
In wacky weather, ideas swarm.

So grab a pen, let laughter flow,
In every line, let mischief grow.
A garden full of quirky plots,
Where stories sprout in funny spots.

First Light of Reflection

In a mirror of dew, the morning's here,
A caterpillar snorts, its bum's sincere.
It stretches wide, prepares to boast,
But slips on leaves; oh, what a toast!

The sun peeks in, with a cheeky grin,
While birds break out their morning din.
"Did you see that fall? What a sight!"
Squeaked a squirrel laughing with delight.

The world giggles as shadows stretch,
A little turtle learns to sketch.
With clumsy strokes and half a plan,
It draws a pizza; what a silly span!

In every glance and every grin,
The dawn reveals the fun within.
As laughter rolls beneath the trees,
Reflections glint in playful breeze.

A Journey through Pages

Once upon a time, or so they say,
A book tried to dance but fell away.
With pages flipping, a windy twirl,
It shouted, "Whee! I'm quite the whirl!"

Heroes hid behind cardboard shields,
While villains plotted in cotton fields.
But every quest took a funny turn,
As pages rippled with tales to learn.

Monsters laughed at their own odd rhymes,
While wizards miscast their spells sometimes.
A dragon sang off-key, what a plight,
And knights slipped on their armor, so tight!

So read aloud, let giggles bloom,
This story's one unpredictable room.
In every chapter, fun extends,
Where laughter's ink never needs to end.

Young Echoes on the Breeze

The whispers of youth dance on the wind,
A frog croaks loudly, as if it grinned.
It croons to flowers, with leaps so spry,
"Let's make some noise! Come on, oh my!"

Butterflies flutter, they join the fun,
With colors bright, they shine like the sun.
In playful circles, they twirl and spin,
Each echo rings with a joyful din.

On sandy shores, where giggles play,
The crabs do the cha-cha, hip-hip-hooray!
While seagulls squawk their silly themes,
In the symphony of sunlit dreams.

So let the breezes tickle your ears,
And share a laugh to lighten your fears.
In every valley and peak you find,
Echoes of joy and fun intertwine.

From Roots to Rhyme

A seed once sown, it stretched so wide,
It wanted to dance, and not just slide.
With roots that giggled, branches that swayed,
It started to rhyme on a sunlit parade.

The clouds above laughed, joined in the cheer,
As blossoms burst out, a colorful sphere.
Its leaves spun tales of whimsical dreams,
Of squirrels in costumes and bubbling streams.

A breeze would whisper, 'Oh, what a sight!'
As flowers would twirl in pure delight.
Each petal a verse, each stem a new line,
This garden of giggles was simply divine.

With bees that recited their buzz in the air,
A melody rang, without a care.
The garden in bloom, laughter was prime,
Oh, the fun that flowed from roots to rhyme!

Chronicles of the Young Heart

In a kingdom where socks never matched,
Lived a young heart whose dreams were hatched.
It rolled on the grass, feeling quite free,
And penned down its thoughts with glee.

With crayons of sunshine and clouds made of fluff,
It scribbled tales, oh, the woofs and the puffs!
The squirrel built castles, the ants wore capes,
As giggles exploded like tasty red grapes.

Adventures unspooled like yarn on a ball,
Each mischief crafted to enthrall.
A pirate in search of a patty for lunch,
With jellybeans bouncing at every crunch.

With every heartbeat, the stories grew tall,
In a world where socks never matched at all.
Oh, the chronicles penned were silly yet sweet,
A canvas of chaos and good-hearted beat!

In the Arms of Discovery

With a map made of candy and dreams spun of cheese,
A curious spirit swayed in the breeze.
It hopped on a toad that wore a fine hat,
And cheered as it found a new way to chat.

They roamed through the fields of bright polka-dots,
Past giggling gnomes and dancing robots.
Each step was a puzzle, a riddle, a jest,
In the arms of discovery, they found the best.

A river of chocolate, oh what a treat,
The more they explored, the more they'd repeat!
With laughter like bubbles, they skipped on the way,
In a world full of wonders, where silly gnomes play.

Curiosity sparkled, a wild little flame,
Every twist of fate was a whimsical game.
Oh, the joy of it all, with giggles combined,
In the arms of discovery, magic was blind!

A Symphony of New Words

In a land where words waltzed in pairs,
A symphony cranked up, filling the airs.
With giggles like trumpets and sighs that hum,
A merry little tune began to strum.

Each noun wore a hat, each verb danced around,
As colors of syntax swirled in a sound.
The adverbs twirled like leaves in full flight,
Creating a chaos that felt so right.

Exclamations jumped, like popcorn in heat,
While metaphors wobbled on wiggly feet.
A cacophony of laughter mixed with delight,
In a symphony where every word took flight.

So join in the chorus, let voices unite,
In this crazy orchestra of pure childlike light.
For the joy of the language, it's a wondrous spree,
A melody crafted for you and for me!

Fresh Pages in Bloom

In a world of pen and ink,
A toddler's nose began to think,
With scribbles grand, a joy to find,
It wrote of socks and cheese, entwined.

The paper laughed, it danced with glee,
As misplaced words climbed up a tree,
A raindrop fell, it made a splash,
And turned the sonnet into trash!

Each line a giggle, each phrase a cheer,
A poet's plan was quite unclear,
With crayons wild, and humor bold,
The budding bard's tales will unfold.

So let them write in playful tune,
With every word, the sun and moon,
In gardens where the giggles bloom,
A party held in every room!

Echoes of New Beginnings

A baby bird attempts to sing,
But all that comes is 'buzz' and 'ding',
It flaps its wings, it trips a bit,
And lands right on the poet's wit!

A pencil wiggles, starts to dance,
With jokes that make the garden prance,
Each verse a tumble, each rhyme a lark,
As wit takes flight with quite a spark!

The blooms all chuckle in delight,
With every line, the plants unite,
In every petal, laughter swirls,
While butterflies share silly twirls.

Let words be wild, let verses play,
With silly tales that shout hooray,
New beginnings, full of cheer,
With every joke, springtime draws near!

The Poetic Seedling

A sprout with dreams of being grand,
Wrote poems in the local sand,
It rhymed with worms and ants, oh my!
As laughter echoed from the sky!

With raindrops giggling on its head,
It penned a tale of a frog in bed,
With every line, a silly twist,
In gardens where the daisies kissed.

"Oh look!" it wrote, "a cow just flew!"
"And danced a jig with a shoe or two!"
The flowers blushed, they waved their leaves,
As humor sprouted, stopping thieves!

So here we cheer for every seed,
That plants a dream, or funny deed,
In every laugh, the joy will thrive,
A world where fun and words arrive!

Verses in the Spring Air

The flowers talked, a chatty crew,
They whispered tales of sunshine rue,
With every line, a chuckle bright,
As bumblebees took their flight!

A comical breeze began to tease,
It swooped through branches, rocked the trees,
With giggles swirling in the air,
The seedlings laughed without a care.

In sunny spots, the verses sprout,
With silly hats and lots of clout,
The ants all joined, a marching band,
Oh what a sight, it's quite unplanned!

So let it bloom, this joyful cheer,
With silly rhymes that bring good beer,
For in the spring, we dance and sing,
A funny tale of everything!

Inspired by Nature's Call

In the garden where daisies dance,
A kooky bug takes a daring chance.
He believes he can sing like a star,
But sounds more like a rusty car.

Bees buzz loudly, trying to hum,
While butterflies laugh, saying, "Oh, come!"
A caterpillar rolls, all in a spin,
Wiggling around with a toothy grin.

The tree branches sway with a chuckle,
As squirrels perform a wild shuffle.
Nature's stage is pure, silly fun,
Where every creature is number one!

But in this jolly woodland so bright,
Even the mushrooms break out in light.
Toadstools caper, sprouting their rhymes,
In this whimsical place, joy chimes!

Petals and Poems

Petals flutter like laughter in air,
As roses wear hats like fine folk, with flair.
Daisies take bets on who'll first bloom,
While tulips are dressed in their Sunday gloom.

The lily pads giggle, playing croquet,
While frogs in tuxedos shout, "Hooray!"
Each bloom with a verse that tickles the sky,
Crafts silly sonnets as breezes pass by.

Worms write sonnets in earthy delight,
While worms are our poets who wiggle and write.
With ink made of dew and a quill: a blade,
They scribble their lines while in mud, they wade.

But be careful, dear friend, while walking near,
A flower may burst forth with laughter and cheer!
Spouting verses till all of us moan,
Creating a garden that feels like home!

Harmonies of the Heart

In the park, the pigeons sing out loud,
Voicing their gossip, feeling quite proud.
With each coo and flap, they crack a joke,
While nearby, the puppies chase a smoke.

Old trees shake leaves, joining the fun,
While squirrels play chess beneath the sun.
A thunder of giggles dances in air,
As laughter erupts without any care.

Each laugh a note in our carefree choir,
A melody played as hearts grow higher.
The sun winks down, feeling the play,
In this land of chuckles where we sway.

Crickets with fiddles ignite the night,
Strumming their tunes, oh, what a sight!
From whispers of leaves to roars of delight,
Our harmony plays till the morning light!

Bursting into Song

One shy bud woke with a ticklish grin,
Not yet a flower, but aiming to win.
It cleared its throat with a flourish of glee,
And suggested, "Let's sing, come join me!"

With petals all fluffed and pollen on paws,
The choir of blooms opened their jaws.
Daisies sang duets, fresh and so bold,
While violets joined in with stories retold.

A bumblebee buzzed, a raucous delight,
Joining the fun with its rhythmic flight.
It hummed a tune that made flowers sway,
Causing ants nearby to dance in the fray.

But the daisies giggled, feeling so spry,
As a breeze whispered secrets that made petals fly.
And with every chuckle, every sweet song,
Nature's own party carried us along!

A Canvas of Words

In a land where rhymes like to play,
Paints all the words in a silly way.
With a stroke of a quill, they dance around,
Making laughter a joyous sound.

The letters jump, do a crazy jig,
Silly sentences are getting big.
Puns and jokes, they start to twirl,
In this colorful, chaotic swirl.

Brushing up verses with a wink,
Every phrase makes you stop and think.
As hues of humor splatter wide,
Each moment, a funny thought to hide.

So dip your brush, let it flow,
In this vibrant world, join the show.
For every stanza brings a cheer,
And giggles echo, loud and clear.

Metaphors in the Meadow

In the meadow where the metaphors grow,
With daisies that rhyme and sunflowers that glow.
A punny butterfly flits on by,
Tickling the clouds in the sunny sky.

The trees tell tales with their whispering leaves,
While rabbits weave puns that nobody believes.
A carrot hero hops with delight,
In this world, everything feels just right.

Each flower buzzes with a cheeky grin,
Laughing together as the day begins.
With similes bouncing like soft little beds,
And laughter sprouting from all their heads.

So wander with words, let your heart race,
In the meadow's warm and comical space.
For every chuckle is a seed you sow,
In this quaint little garden where humor will grow.

Words Taking Root

Words are seeds in a comical ground,
Planting puns that can spin around.
They curl and twirl in the breezy air,
With each little laugh, they find a pair.

Giggles sprout from tales all tied,
Where metaphors play, and jokes reside.
The garden of phrases begins to bloom,
Filling the world with laughter and room.

So water your thoughts, let them explode,
In this vibrant, expressive abode.
As humor takes root in the heart's warm nest,
Every chuckle's a treasure, every joke's a fest.

Soon fruits of fun will hang from the trees,
Plucking the giggles will be a breeze.
With each tasty word, you'll wear a grin,
In this field of laughter, let's all spin!

Flight of the Young Muse

A young muse dances with feathers of cheer,
Writing bright tales that everyone can hear.
On clouds of giggles, she takes to flight,
Painting the skies with sheer delight.

With a wink and a nod, she skips through the air,
Spilling her laughter without a care.
Comedic spells twirl around in her wake,
As mischief and joy make the world quake.

She rides on the backs of the jolly breeze,
Spreading her humor with the greatest of ease.
In each little whisper, a chuckle is found,
As words fly high and spin all around.

So let the young muse take you away,
To a land where nobody has a gray day.
With each tickled thought, you'll rise and glide,
In this joyful journey, let laughter be your guide.

Grafting Imagery

In a garden where words take flight,
Tangled vines yearn for the light.
A poet's quill, a curious bee,
Buzzing around a comedic spree.

Oh, the tomatoes tell jokes at noon,
While carrots dance to a silly tune.
The daisies giggle, heads all a-bob,
Imagining what it means to blab!

In this patch, there's no need for rules,
Where eggplants try to outsmart the fools.
Each verse is a seed, each punchline a bud,
Sprouting fresh laughter from deep in the mud.

So come lie down in the grassy bed,
And share all the stories that swirl in your head.
For in this garden of whimsical cheer,
There's sunshine and mirth, and no room for fear.

Garden of Untold Stories

In a plot where whispers roam free,
Lively tales hang from each tree.
The squirrels snicker at the crows,
As the garden's drama continuously grows.

Roses play poker beneath the moon,
While daisies waltz in a wild cartoon.
Story seeds scatter in the breeze,
Planting giggles among the trees.

Each leaf has a grinning tale to tell,
Of misplaced shoes and a cat named Mel.
The veggies gather, plotting their play,
In this patch, the weird rules the day!

So grab your spade and dig up a line,
Pull out a laugh from the roots of the vine.
For in this garden, both wild and fun,
Stories bloom brighter under the sun.

Rhymes Awakening

Awake, awaken, the rhymes jiggle,
Squirrels chuckle and feet begin to wriggle.
From top of the hill to the root down below,
A song bursts forth, ready to grow.

The daisies chorus in a comic tune,
While shadows dance with a playful swoon.
The sun beams in with a wink in his eye,
And tickles the tulips, oh my, oh my!

Jokes spill out from the earth's happy seams,
Where laughter is part of the soil's sweet dreams.
A garden of rhymes, a riotous spree,
Come frolic with poetry, wild and carefree.

So pull up a chair made of clashing words,
Where feelings of joy take flight like birds.
Let the rhymes awaken your giggle and grin,
In the garden where mischief and bliss always win.

The Verse Unfolds

In the quiet nook where the verses bloom,
Giggles slip out like lifting a broom.
A sunflower whispers a silly decree,
"Let's toast to the plants and their frolicsome glee!"

The roots tie together in serendipitous pranks,
As the ferns outshine the cautious pranks.
Each petal a note in the chorus we sing,
Echoing moments, oh, what joy they bring!

Adventures emerge, like a sprout from the ground,
Where beans do a jig, in whirlwinds profound.
The farmer chuckles, juggling seeds in the air,
With stories that tickle, beyond compare.

So heed the laughter as the verses unfold,
Tales of the garden, both silly and bold.
For in this realm of whimsy and cheer,
Every word plants a smile year after year.

Experiments in Expression

In the lab of rhyme, I mix and stir,
With crazy metaphors that occasionally blur.
I spilled some puns, they slipped on the floor,
Now my verses giggle and beg for more!

My rhymes are like socks, all mismatched and bright,
Some end up in laundry, lost, out of sight.
I'm baking with humor, a dash of delight,
Who knew that wordplay could take flight?

I'll juggle my stanzas, toss lines through the air,
Like a clown in a circus, I hardly despair.
Each twist and each turn, a laugh in my quest,
For jest is my goal, let's have some fun, at best!

So here's to the chaos, the hullabaloo,
Where expressing my thoughts means breaking some rules.
With laughter my compass, I take off in glee,
This madcap adventure is just for me!

Leafy Whispers of Poetry

Under the shade of a grapevine's stare,
I found some words that just didn't care.
They rustled and giggled, with leaves all a-flutter,
Claiming my verses should write in peanut butter!

The flowers chimed in, 'Let's rhyming be fun!
With petals for confetti, let's rhyme 'til we're done!'
But bees started buzzing, 'What's all this fuss?'
Do I hear a sonnet? Or was that a bus?

Oh, squirrels crack nuts while they gather their lines,
I overheard acorns making rhyming designs.
"Let's pen a poem!" they squeaked with delight,
While birds chirped the chorus, "We'll sing through the night!"

As laughter took root in the garden of thought,
Every twig whispered secrets that just couldn't be taught.
In this leafy realm where nonsense blooms free,
I create silly sonnets, just you wait and see!

Ember and Bloom

In a garden of giggles, I planted a seed,
Nurtured with laughter and a pinch of some greed.
It sprouted a stem full of jokes and surprise,
With petals like teacups, they winked with their eyes.

The embers of fun flickered bright in the night,
As moonbeams arranged a delightful sight.
"Tell us a joke!" the daisies all cried,
"My petals are ticklish, I'll not be denied!"

With verses ablaze like a campfire's chat,
I whispered sweet sonnets, while insects went splat.
The blooms broke out laughing, with rhymes that took flight,
Making memories bright as the stars filled the night.

So here in my patch, where the silly things roam,
With embers and blooms, I've found my true home.
Together they dance in this whimsical space,
Where laughter and poetry intertwine with grace!

Serenade of New Beginnings

With a wink and a nod, I strummed my guitar,
Singing silly anthems beneath the bright star.
Each note played a ditty, a whimsical tune,
To celebrate nonsense as dreams break the moon!

My words took a stroll on a bright, sunny day,
Dressed in polka dots that just wanted to play.
New beginnings in verses, with humor so keen,
Like tickled pink fairies, they danced in between!

The balloons whispered secrets, they laughed with delight,

As I juggled my rhymes under soft, shining light.
Each stanza a cake, each line frosted sweet,
I served up a feast that was hard to beat!

In this serenade, let mirth be the guide,
With each note I play, joy will take a stride.
Together we'll laugh, we'll bloom as we sing,
In this dance of new moments, let happiness spring!

Blossoming Lines

In a garden of rhyme, I plant my words,
With puns like petals, just waiting to burst.
I water my quips with laughter and cheer,
Each chuckle a bloom, delightful and dear.

My metaphors sprout like weeds in the sun,
They dance in the breeze, oh what silly fun!
A simile here, an alliteration there,
These flowers of language grow everywhere.

I pick a few verses, all jesters in line,
Each one a cactus, sharp but divine.
Yet, watch for the thorns, they've sprouted with glee,
A jab or a laugh, just to keep it funny.

Soon bees will come buzzing, attracted by me,
In-stinctiv'ly sweet, they're singing with glee.
The buds in my mind are now fully in bloom,
With laughter and joy filling up every room.

The Poet's Awakening

Awake with a giggle, I grab for my pen,
In dreams of wordplay, I scribble again.
The rooster's a haiku, the cat's a free verse,
Each creature beside me, a line to converse.

My breakfast is metaphors, sizzling on toast,
With scrambled sentiments, I munch on the most.
A sprinkle of humor, dear syrupy laughs,
As I write with delight, on this morning that puffs.

The flowers are typing, with petals aglow,
They tweet out intentions, while putting on a show.
I'm chuckling at rhymes that seem fluffed up with cream,
A poet's awakening, as bright as a dream.

Oh what fun it is, to dance through the lines,
With laughter that frolics and merrily shines.
Each verse is a tickle, a playful delight,
In this world of whimsy, I write through the night.

Notes from the Flowerbed

Among blooms and giggles, my quill takes a stroll,
Planting notes that flutter, like leaves in a bowl.
With petals for paper, I scribble away,
In a garden of chuckles, I'm here to stay.

Each flower a stanza, with color and flair,
While bees buzz my music, filling the air.
A daisy's a punchline, a rose a refrain,
With humor as sunshine, joy can't be tamed.

The worms read my verses, all wriggly and wise,
They chuckle at puns, 'til they roll with surprise.
I write down their laughter, in dirt with a grin,
These notes from the flowerbed, where poetry begins.

So listen, dear friend, to the rustling leaves,
Each laugh is a blossom that none can believe.
In this funny garden, let's plant seeds of cheer,
And watch as the humor grows year after year.

Growing Words

With a trowel of wit, I dig up some rhymes,
Nurturing seedlings of laughter, in climes.
The sun shines on laughter, watering the cheer,
As my garden of giggles flourishes here.

Each word is a sprout, in the soil of the night,
Reaching for humor, stretching out for the light.
I prune back the doubts with a snip and a snort,
As I harvest my verses, a gleeful report.

Pollinating puns as the butterflies dance,
On petals of verses, they sway and enhance.
The whimsical weeds, they make quite a scene,
A patch of pure folly, of giggles so green.

Oh, laughter is growing, it's a marvelous sight,
In the garden of joy, where words take to flight.
So let's sow our absurdity, let the fun start,
In this playful abode, it's a giggling heart.

Crafting Shadows and Light

In the garden of fables, I trip and I fall,
Chasing whispers of laughter, I giggle and sprawl.
My dreams are like shadows, they dance in the sun,
Crafting stories from giggles, oh isn't this fun?

With a wink and a nod, I summon the breeze,
A parade of odd creatures, all hungry for cheese.
They prance with a purpose, so silly and spry,
Who knew that my quirks could take flight in the sky?

I scribble my antics on leaves made of gold,
Each word a wild rabbit, so cheeky and bold.
With laughter as ink, and joy as my page,
The world is a stage, and life is the rage!

So let's spin a yarn, let's tumble and roll,
With shadows and light, let's dance to our soul.
As we craft tales together, we tickle the night,
In this garden of nonsense, everything's right!

Sprouts of Imagination

In the field of daydreams where giggles are sown,
Sprouts of imagination begin to be grown.
They wiggle and wriggle, those thoughts in my head,
Turned upside down, they bounce out of bed!

A tomato by twilight claims it's a star,
While carrots wear top hats and play air guitar.
They dance in the sunlight, they twirl and they sway,
Sprouting up new ideas to cheer up the day!

I patch quilt my stories on breezes so light,
Each thought is a kite taking off in delight.
With whimsy as fuel, we'll soar through the sky,
Who knew that our laughter could take us so high?

So come join the frolic, let imagination bloom,
Turn frowns into giggles, let joy fill the room.
In this silly garden where dreams intertwine,
Sprouts of imagination transform into rhyme!

Written in the Dew

In the early morn, as the grass wears a dress,
I find little whispers of stories to express.
With dew drops like diamonds, I capture the fun,
Each droplet an echo of laughter undone.

Oh, the squirrels are gossiping, so quick on their toes,
While flowers are cheering for how well it grows.
I pen down their tales, as a breeze starts to hum,
With rhymes that can tickle the wisest of tongues!

Breezy thoughts scatter like fireflies in flight,
Their glow spells out secrets that sparkle at night.
From petals of daisies, silly poems leap,
Written in the dew, oh, the joy oh so deep!

So gather 'round softly as dawn lights the way,
With giggles and whispers, let's start off this day.
In the world made of dew, where laughter is free,
Every drop holds a story just waiting for me!

Tendrils of Thought

With tendrils of thought, I climb through the haze,
Exploring the nooks of my colorful maze.
A noodle of nonsense wraps round my old shoe,
Saying, "Join in the fun! We've got much more to do!"

Oh, the clouds are my canvas, I splash and I play,
With a brush made of giggles, I brighten the gray.
And flowers with voices start singing my song,
In this symphony of smiles, it's where I belong!

As I twirl in the tangle of whimsies and cheer,
Each knot in my thoughts whispers, "Stay close, my dear."
For in this wild garden, imagination is king,
With tendrils of thought, oh, the joy that we bring!

Let's leap on the breeze, my tall tales we'll weave,
In this laughter-filled land, oh, it's hard to believe!
So come, let's get tangled and joyfully sway,
With tendrils of thought, we'll giggle away!

The Birth of Verses

In a garden of giggles, rhymes begin,
A tree of odd thoughts, let the chaos spin.
With a pen like a squirrel, dashing about,
Chasing lines that tease and jump all about.

Words sprout like daisies, colorful and bright,
Puns flying high like a kite at first light.
Each stanza a fruit, ripe for the pick,
Juicy and sweet, a poetic trick.

Laughter wraps around every phrase in flight,
As metaphors dance beneath the moonlight.
Once shy in the shade, now bold in the sun,
A jester in ink, writing just for fun.

With each silly verse, the laughter grows loud,
Witty little lines, I'm so very proud.
A birth of a poem, oh what a delight,
In this comical garden, everything's right.

Constellations of Thought and Bloom

Stars wink like words in the dark of night,
A cosmic giggle causing quite the fright.
Ideas twinkle, flying all around,
Like a juggling clown, they tumble and bound.

Thoughts scatter like seeds from a playful breeze,
Landing in places that make one say 'geez!'
Each one blooming into something quite fun,
A galaxy of laughter, all said and done.

Planets of puns orbit joyfully near,
Spinning around, bringing forth lots of cheer.
With every new line, a star is reborn,
In this sky of humor, we happily adorn.

So let's raise a glass to this wondrous space,
Where silly ideas dance with a comical grace.
In the universe of giggles, we gleefully glide,
Amongst these bright thoughts, we take a wild ride.

Petal-Pushed Phrases

In this garden of giggles, words bloom so bright,
Petal-pushed phrases ready for flight.
Each line a flower, unfurling with glee,
Tickling the fancy of you and of me.

With quips like bees buzzing from flower to flower,
Crafting a rainbow in this whimsical hour.
A dash of absurdity, sprinkle some cheer,
In the laughter-filled garden, all is sincere.

Whimsical whispers ride on warm breezes,
Playing hide and seek, just like little teasers.
A bouquet of madness wrapped snug in a rhyme,
We frolic in verses, enjoying our time.

So grab a handful of joy from this patch,
Where funny ideas come ready to hatch.
Each line is a petal, each word a delight,
In this playful garden, let's giggle tonight.

An Orchard of Dreams

Wandering through trees, where thoughts intertwine,
An orchard of whimsy, where jokes align.
Branches bend low with berries of fun,
Harvesting laughter, one by one.

Each fruit holds a secret, tucked snug inside,
Biting into punchlines, we can't help but slide.
Giggling like children, we dart to and fro,
In this orchard of dreams, the humor does grow.

Sunshine and silliness dance on the leaves,
With rhymes hanging down, like ripe, golden sheaves.
Plucking warm laughter, we toast to the day,
In this orchard of dreams, come frolic and play.

So let's gather 'round, raise a cheer to the air,
With silly stories and laughter to share.
In this fruitful delight, together we gleam,
Living the magic of whimsical themes.

The Inkling's Serenade

In a garden where giggles thrive,
A pen stumbles, trying to jive.
With ink that dances, spills like tea,
Words trampoline, oh so free!

The daisies laugh, they can't resist,
As rhymes play tag, a twisty twist.
A butterfly winks, "Can you keep up?"
With hiccuping verses in a teacup!

The moon winks down, a playful sprite,
"Write me a sonnet before goodnight!"
But the ink has gone awry, oh dear,
It's more of a squabble than a cheer!

So we frolic in laughter, here we play,
With silly stanzas that lead us astray.
Each line a jiggle, a fun little poke,
In the realm of rhymes, we're all just a joke!

Verses Yet to Bloom

In a pot of soil, ideas sprout,
Some are zany, some just pout.
With each new bloom, a chuckling shout,
What on Earth is this all about?

A cactus claims it's quite the prose,
While daisies giggle at his pose.
"Oh, grow up!" they tease with flair,
But he's got thorns and doesn't care!

An acorn dreams of poetry grand,
But roots are tangled in the sand.
"Just leaf it to me," it starts to cry,
"I'll be mighty oak, just give a try!"

So here we plant our quirky seeds,
Each silly verse fulfills our needs.
In laughter we cultivate our truth,
As jokes sprout wildly, free and uncouth!

Rhyme and Renewal

In the land where silly words renew,
A rhyme rolls by, slipped in a shoe!
The clock chimes funny, tick-tock, tick-tock,
While the jester juggles a comical rock!

The trees bark out, "What's your best pun?"
And echoes chuckle, "This's no fun!"
Yet every leaf shimmies with glee,
As fresh lines wiggle, wild and free!

A squirrel recites a limerick loud,
He's proud of his silly little crowd.
With nuts for lines and acorns for keys,
He serenades all in the breeze!

As laughter blossoms in the air,
It fills our hearts with warmth and care.
In this garden of phrase and jest,
We'll write silly sonnets, never a rest!

Echoes of Untamed Growth

In a field where the wild words roam,
A tumbleweed rolls, far from home.
With hiccups and giggles, they take a dive,
In a chaotic shuffle, they feel alive!

The flowers trade puns, a jesting spree,
While frogs leap high, croaking in glee.
"Take a ribbit!" they quip and croon,
As the daisies giggle, "Time for a tune!"

Bumblebees buzz with a chuckle and sting,
Their rhymes are a flurry, a joyful fling.
They dance in the air, as blossoms sway,
"Pollinate this!" they happily say!

So let's grow wild in this lyrical art,
With echoes of joy to fill every heart.
In the mess of words, we find our way,
A garden of laughter, forever we'll play!

Dreams of a Wordsmith

In the land of rhymes so bright,
A walrus danced by day and night.
With a top hat on his head so tall,
He recited poems to one and all.

A cat in pajamas, fluffy and round,
Played the piano, such a strange sound.
As words spilled from its tiny paws,
The audience cheered, applauding with jaws.

A frog wore glasses, read a book,
Sipping tea from an old, chipped nook.
Each sentence wobbled, then took flight,
And lanterns flickered, dancing with delight.

So if you think being a bard's a bore,
Just peek a little closer at the lore.
For in the world of fanciful dreams,
Even silliness flows in gleams!

Unfurling Lines

A squirrel once penned a tale so grand,
With acorns and nuts, his writing brand.
He scribbled fast with a tiny quill,
And even wrote 'The Nutty Thrill.'

A bear in a tutu threw a dance,
With every step, he took a chance.
His pirouettes left trees all shook,
As friends all gathered to read his book.

A parrot squawked nonsense, loud and clear,
While perched on a poet's shoulder near.
"Polly wants verses!" it wildly called,
Then cackled with laughter, and wildly sprawled.

With every word, the world unwinds,
In the grandest tale that humor finds.
So tip your hat and take a seat,
For the giggling words can't be beat!

The Dawn of a Poet's Heart

A panda woke with ink-stained paws,
Dreaming of writing without a pause.
He dipped his brush in honey sweet,
And painted poems for a tasty treat.

A turtle played catch with a flying cloud,
He tossed it lines, feeling quite proud.
With each snappy throw, the cloud would giggle,
As the turtle clapped, doing a wiggle.

A rabbit with spectacles read all night,
Mixing up tales that brought delight.
When asked for advice on a wordy spout,
He'd blink and proclaim, "Do not forget about carrots!"

So when dawn breaks, hear the laughter ring,
As the world finds joy in the joy of fling.
For in every heart beats a silly tune,
Just waiting to burst, like a birthday balloon!

Petals of Inspiration

A hippo in pink wrote a scrumptious ode,
While sipping a milkshake, it overflowed.
Each stanza dripped with sticky delight,
As laughter bubbled in the warm sunlight.

A flamingo painted with feathers so bright,
Danced on a tablet, quite a sight!
With each pirouette, words sprouted wide,
As giggles erupted, a joyful tide.

A snail sat slow with a pen in tow,
Crafting verses with a splendid flow.
He'd stop to think, oh what a rout,
"I took too long. I'll never get out!"

But every poet knows the deeper truth,
That silly setbacks can yield sweet proof.
In a world of whimsy, laughter's a part,
Where petals of joy bloom in each heart!

Stirrings of Creativity

A mouse with a pen, oh what a sight,
He scribbles and giggles by moon's soft light.
With papers flying, he dances around,
Chasing wild ideas that bounce on the ground.

The cat in the corner gives a loud yawn,
Dreaming of tuna and garden lawn.
But the mouse just laughs and won't back down,
His poems are treasures, he wears a crown.

In the kitchen, he finds some old spice,
Mixing up verses like cakes, oh so nice!
With each verse he bakes, a new flavor appears,
A feast of laughter for all who come near.

So if you see shadows on a warm summer night,
It's just a mouse writing, getting it right!
With quips and some puns, he's filled to the brim,
In a world of his making, it's joy on a whim.

Lyrics Among the Leaves

In the heart of the woods, leaves start to sway,
A squirrel sings tunes in a cheeky display.
With acorns as maracas, he follows the beat,
While chipmunks join in, tapping their feet.

A babbling brook adds its musical flair,
Together they create a loud, merry air.
The sunbeams chuckle, filtering through trees,
As wind whispers jokes, carried on the breeze.

The chorus grows louder, a riotous cheer,
Even grumpy old owls can't help but draw near.
They hoot in confusion, heads start to sway,
Wondering if this is a new kind of play.

So if you're out walking, stop for a glance,
And join in the merriment, give life a chance.
Grab a leaf for a hat, twirl round with glee,
For in nature's own stage, it's a giggle spree!

New Paths of Expression

A snail with a brush paints a trail on the street,
It's modern art, though not quite discreet.
With splatters of color, he makes quite a mess,
Yet claims he's the next big artistic success.

A frog leaps on canvas, leaving green spots,
Each jump a new masterpiece—oh dear, lots!
While bees buzz by, creating a buzz,
Inspiring this slug to create just because.

A kite made of paper gets caught in a tree,
Flapping and flailing, oh what a spree!
The wind takes a laugh at the scene up above,
While artists unite in a display of love.

So embrace your own style, let creativity flow,
Even if it's messy, just let your heart show.
For in this sweet chaos, art finds its way,
And laughter will echo, come join the ballet!

Expressions of New Life

A puppy with papers scribbles notes in a daze,
Chewing on pencils in whimsical ways.
His tail wags wildly, a whirlwind of fun,
Creating a ruckus till the day is done.

With each playful bark, he imagines a rhyme,
Chasing down verses, oh what a climb!
A kitten joins in, pounces on the page,
Turning each stanza into a cat-tastrophe stage.

They form a grand duo, this hilarious pair,
Crafting wild tales without any care.
Paw prints on poetry, fur on the text,
Each line a ramble, what's coming next?

So if you find chaos in your quiet nook,
Just know that the pup is creating a book.
With laughter and joy, they're redefining life,
In a world of fun chaos, away from the strife.

Whispers of a New Dawn

A little bird sang out loud,
Its voice sweet and quite proud.
It tried to impress the sun,
But tripped on a branch – oh what fun!

The flowers danced in the breeze,
Wiggling their stems with such ease.
They giggled at clouds passing by,
Like fluffy sheep in the sky.

A ladybug wore a top hat,
Declaring, "I'm so very fat!"
Its friends rolled their eyes in delight,
Each chuckle echoed in flight.

With a wink, the dawn took its stand,
Painting the sky with its hand.
The world burst forth in bright cheer,
As laughter rang out far and near.

Verses in the Cradle of Spring

Puppies barking, chasing their tails,
A chorus of giggles and happy trails.
The daisies nodding, quite amused,
At the antics of bees so confused.

A frog croaked a tune with flair,
While birds swayed without a care.
The sunlight waltzed on the lake,
Painting ripples for laughter's sake.

A tulip tripped in its bloom,
Spinning round with a grand zoom.
The breeze was a jester, quite spry,
Sending petals up to the sky.

Spring's gallery filled with jest,
Where giggles and blossoms coalesce.
The world spins in this joyful fling,
In the playful cradle of spring.

Ink and Petals

In a garden where stories grow,
A daisy dreams of a poetry show.
With petals like pages, oh so bright,
It scribbles verses under the light.

A butterfly acts like a quill,
Writes sonnets on the windowsill.
While a snail, taking great pride,
Recites his lines with a slow glide.

With ink made of dew and delight,
They compose all day and all night.
A humorous tale of weeds and sun,
A raucous read when spring has begun.

Each flower has its own tale to tell,
Of mischief and laughter as well.
In the garden, both wild and free,
Ink and petals weave joyfully.

Blossoms of Imagination

In the land of whimsical glee,
Where flowers can giggle and trees can see.
A petal decided to play a game,
Daring the wind to call its name.

A charming worm wrote a novel,
About a snail with a traveler's trouble.
Each line curled around with such flair,
Creating a tale with laughs to share.

The tulips wore hats, quite absurd,
To welcome the fanciest bird.
They laughed at a breeze that gave chase,
Each swirl a dance, a joyful embrace.

In fields of imagination's bloom,
Where laughter dispels all gloom.
With every chuckle, joy transcends,
In this playful world where fun never ends.

Whispers in the Green

In a forest so dense, with chatter and cheer,
Frogs in tuxedos make music quite near.
Squirrels wearing glasses take notes on a tree,
While owls with their wisdom sip tea happily.

A rabbit recites, though he's slightly unfit,
His audience giggles, yet urges him to quit.
The trees take a bow, their branches all sway,
As critters declare, "That was quite the display!"

The daisies all chuckle, they dance all around,
Mice open a bakery, with cookies profound.
The laughter erupts and the jokes take their flight,
In this forest of jesters, all feels just right.

So next time you wander where wild things convene,
Listen closely to laughter that's seldom seen.
For humor's a treasure, both subtle and bright,
In the whispers of green, oh, what a delight!

Impressions on a Fresh Canvas

A painter like no other, he's always absurd,
With brushes and giggles, he transforms the world.
His palette a circus, with colors that shout,
Each stroke brings a smile; there's never a doubt.

He splatters the canvas with jellybean hues,
A giraffe wears a top hat, amusing the blues.
The trees wear pajamas and dance with bold grace,
In this wacky creation, there's always a place.

Curly lines twist around in a dizzying spin,
All shapes become silly, where nonsense begins.
The people just laugh, as they join the parade,
Taking joy in each brushstroke that's freely displayed.

With every new layer, the whimsy expands,
A tale of delight flows from clever hands.
In art, there's a magic, a giggle-filled trance,
Where joy finds its rhythm, and laughter will dance!

Eager Ink

A quill in the moonlight, it stirs with a grin,
Waking up the pages, enticing the whim.
With paper as canvas, it scribbles away,
Each sonnet a tickle, a humorous play.

Ink blots like hiccups, they dance on the page,
As characters leap out, funny, wise, and sage.
A cactus in slippers reads poems aloud,
While blobs of bright color throw laughter the crowd.

Ink drips like giggles, making puddles of cheer,
The pen skips and hops, as if it can hear.
Witty lines tumble, each one gets a round,
In the fables of scribbles, pure joy will abound.

So gather your stories, let your thoughts race,
For in every line, there's a merry embrace.
With the power of laughter and playful design,
The ink flows like magic, creating divine!

Underneath the Surface

Beneath the calm waters, where secrets reside,
Fish wear party hats, and dolphins take pride.
An octopus juggles with laughter and flair,
While turtles in tuxedos float without care.

Seaweed is chatting, with crabs in a jest,
Each wave is a rhythm, a playful request.
The clownfish hold court, making jokes, quite grand,
As bubbles rise up, like confetti from sand.

Coral reefs giggle, with colors so bright,
As starfish make wishes under soft moonlight.
A pirate with treasure—doubloons made of cheese—
Delights all the fishes with tales that tease.

In this underwater world, where fun comes alive,
Every creature rejoices, where laughter will thrive.
So dive in and explore, where the funny's a charm,
For under the surface, there's friendship and warm!

www.ingramcontent.com/pod-product-compliance
Lightning Source LLC
Chambersburg PA
CBHW071845160426
43209CB00003B/425